D0758975

ITHDRAWN

POISON DART FROGS

BY LISA OWINGS

BELLWETHER MEDIA • MINNEAPOLIS, MN

This edition first published in 2012 by Bellwether Media, Inc.

No part of this publication may be reproduced in whole or in part without written permission of the publisher.
For information regarding permission, write to Bellwether Media, Inc., Attention: Permissions Department,
5357 Penn Avenue South, Minneapolis, MN 55419.

Library of Congress Cataloging-in-Publication Data

Owings, Lisa.
 Poison dart frogs / by Lisa Owings.
    p. cm. – (Pilot Books. Nature's deadliest)
 Includes bibliographical references and index.
 Summary: "Fascinating images accompany information about poison dart frogs. The combination of high-interest
subject matter and narrative text is intended for students in grades 3 through 7"–Provided by publisher.
 ISBN 978-1-60014-668-8 (hardcover : alk. paper)
 1. Dendrobatidae–Juvenile literature. I. Title.
 QL668.E233O95 2012
 597.87'7–dc22   2011014725

Text copyright © 2012 by Bellwether Media, Inc. PILOT BOOKS and associated logos are trademarks and/or registered
trademarks of Bellwether Media, Inc. SCHOLASTIC, CHILDREN'S PRESS, and associated logos are trademarks and/or
registered trademarks of Scholastic Inc.

Printed in the United States of America, North Mankato, MN.

080111   1187

CONTENTS

A Deadly Weapon

In the shade of the Colombian rain forest, the air
is cool and damp. Manuelito Maia, a member of
the Emberá tribe, emerges from his hut with a basket
and a handful of leaves. These are the only things
he will need to capture the most poisonous frogs
in the world. Maia walks slowly through the forest
and keeps his eyes on the ground. A small, bright
yellow frog hops across his path. He moves toward
the frog and uses a leaf to carefully pick it up. It is
easy to catch because it is not used to running from
predators. Maia drops the frog and the leaf into his
basket and ties the lid shut. He continues his search,
and it isn't long before he has many golden poison
dart frogs inside the basket. This will be more than
enough. Maia whistles happily as he returns to the
village with his catch.

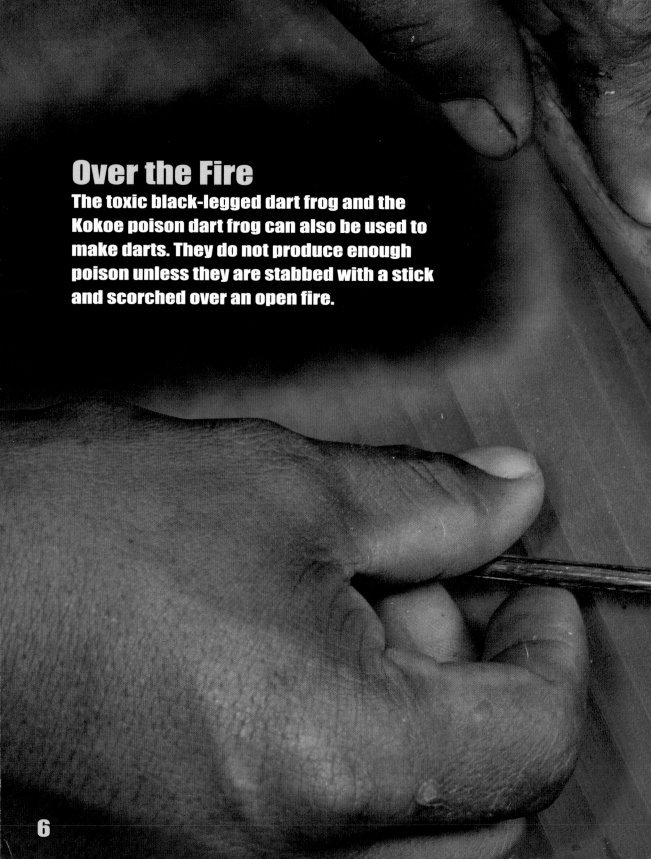

Over the Fire

The toxic black-legged dart frog and the Kokoe poison dart frog can also be used to make darts. They do not produce enough poison unless they are stabbed with a stick and scorched over an open fire.

Maia sets the basket of frogs in a shady spot outside his hut. He goes inside to collect the darts he made a few days ago. He also brings out a **plantain**, a stick, and more leaves. Maia opens the basket just enough for one yellow frog to peek out. He is careful not to touch the frog's skin. It is covered in deadly poison. He uses leaves to pick up the frog and place it on the ground. He lays his stick over the frog to keep it from hopping away. Then Maia picks up a dart and rolls its narrow tip across the frog's back. After applying poison to two more darts, Maia lets the frog go. It takes a few moments to recover before hopping back into the forest. Maia pushes the **blunt** ends of his darts into the soft flesh of the plantain. He reaches for the next golden frog.

Tiny Killer
The amount of golden dart frog poison needed to kill a human is roughly equal to two grains of table salt.

After a few hours in the hot sun, the poison has dried on the tips of the darts. Maia pulls them out of the plantain and puts all but one in his **quiver**. With his **blowgun** loaded, he is ready to join the hunt. He and a few other men from his tribe move silently through the forest. Maia spots the dark fur of a monkey. He brings the blowgun to his lips. With a puff of air, the dart shoots toward its target. The monkey is hit! It is no match for the poison from the tiny yellow frog. The monkey dies in seconds and crashes to the ground. Maia picks it up, careful not to touch the dart poking through its skin. The Emberá men celebrate as they carry their kill back to the village. They can look forward to a good meal tonight.

Pretty Poison

Every poison dart frog has skin that oozes poison. A few **Amerindian** tribes use the frog poison to make poison darts. This is how these frogs got their name. About 200 kinds of poison dart frogs live throughout the warm, wet regions of South and Central America. Most poison dart frogs have bright patterns of red, orange, or yellow on their bodies. Some are green or blue. They evolved this bright coloring to warn predators to stay away. This is known as **aposematism**.

All poison dart frogs are small. The largest are around 3 inches (7.6 centimeters) long. The tiniest measure only half an inch (1.3 centimeters). Don't let their small size and pretty colors fool you. These frogs are some of the deadliest animals on Earth.

poison dart frog territory =

Dart Frog Dads

A dart frog dad carries each individual tadpole on his back until he finds a safe pool of water where it can grow.

Most poison dart frogs are toxic enough to harm or kill snakes, spiders, and other animals. A few are deadly even to humans. However, poison dart frogs only use their deadly toxins for defense. They are not able to inject poison into another animal. Rather, dart frogs **secrete** poison when they feel threatened. Snakes or other predators unfamiliar with dart frogs might try to take a bite. It would be their last mistake. The poison would already be at work before they spit out the bad-tasting frog. The predator would be dead in seconds. Most predators see the bright colors and know to stay away. The frogs hop around freely during the day because few animals dare to come near them.

Copycats

Aposematism works so well to keep hungry predators away that other frogs are using it, too. Many non-poisonous frogs have developed bright coloring that tricks predators into thinking they are poisonous.

Time to Kill

The poisons secreted by the golden poison dart frog remain deadly for a long time. A dart tipped with this poison is still deadly a year later.

The golden poison dart frog has the deadliest poison of any **amphibian**. Some believe it is the most poisonous animal on Earth. It lives only in a small area of the Colombian rain forest. Golden poison dart frogs were the first to be used for poison darts. Members of the Emberá tribe carefully roll the tips of their darts across the backs of these **lethal** frogs. The secretions of a single golden poison dart frog are strong enough to kill more than ten adult humans. People have died from just touching a golden poison dart frog in the wild.

Trail of Death

Golden poison dart frogs can kill even when they are not present. They leave a trail of deadly poison wherever they go. Dogs, chickens, and other animals have died after coming in contact with objects touched by a golden poison dart frog.

black-legged
dart frog

The golden poison dart frog shares its deadly reputation with the black-legged dart frog and the Kokoe poison dart frog. These three frogs produce **batrachotoxins**, the most powerful toxins in nature. These toxins affect the heart and the **nervous system**. They cause muscle **contractions** when they enter the bloodstream. The contractions cause a victim's heart and lungs to stop working. Death comes within minutes. There is no known **antidote** for this poison. Though the frogs that produce batrachotoxins are the deadliest, all poison dart frogs secrete dangerous toxins.

Unlike most poisonous animals, dart frogs do not make their poison. Scientists believe their diet consists of insects that eat poisonous plants. Dart frogs are **immune** to these plant poisons. Instead, they are able to put them to use for their own protection.

Poison Source

Batrachotoxin means "frog poison." However, frogs are not the only creatures that use batrachotoxins. A few kinds of birds in New Guinea were found to produce the same poison. Scientists believe the poison comes from beetles the birds like to eat.

Kokoe
poison dart frog

Harmful and Helpful

Poison dart frogs are beautiful animals. People can observe them in the wild as long as they take care not to touch them. People should always wear gloves when they handle poison dart frogs. Used gloves should be removed carefully and thrown into a sealed container.

Dart frog poison can get into the blood through tiny cuts or wounds. People who touch a poison dart frog by accident should seek medical attention right away. It is critical to wash the poison off immediately, being careful not to spread the toxins to other parts of the body.

Poison or Pet?

Many people keep poison dart frogs as pets. Pet dart frogs are not poisonous because their diets are different from frogs in the wild. However, few dart frogs like to be handled. Their delicate skin is easily damaged.

Poison dart frogs play an important role in the rain forest and beyond. In the rain forest, they eat millions of insects that damage plants. Dart frog poison may also end up saving lives. Scientists are using it to develop muscle relaxers, painkillers, and other powerful medicines. There may be many other uses for dart frog poison yet to be discovered.

Despite their importance, the number of poison dart frogs in the wild is decreasing. They are losing their homes as rain forests are cut down for wood and farmland. As we learn more about these mysterious and dangerous creatures, we may find that the health of both rain forests and humans depends on them.

Glossary

Amerindian—people originally from North, Central, or South America

amphibian—an animal with a body temperature that is the same as its surroundings; amphibians live in water and on land.

antidote—a substance that stops a poison from working

aposematism—the use of bright colors to warn predators to stay away

batrachotoxins—deadly poisons secreted by a few kinds of poison dart frogs; batrachotoxins are the most poisonous substances found in nature.

blowgun—a long wooden tube through which a dart is blown; blowguns are traditional hunting weapons of the Emberá people.

blunt—not sharp

contractions—the shortening or tensing of muscles

immune—not affected by

lethal—deadly

nervous system—a system of the body; the brain, spinal cord, and nerves make up the nervous system.

plantain—a banana-like tropical fruit

quiver—a pouch used to hold darts or arrows while hunting

secrete—to release liquids; poison dart frogs secrete poison through their skin.

To Learn More

At the Library

Bredeson, Carmen. *Poison Dart Frogs Up Close*. Berkeley Heights, N.J.: Enslow Elementary, 2009.

Fridell, Ron. *The Search for Poison-Dart Frogs*. New York, N.Y.: Franklin Watts, 2001.

Ganeri, Anita. *Poison Dart Frog*. Chicago, Ill.: Heinemann Library, 2011.

On the Web

Learning more about poison dart frogs is as easy as 1, 2, 3.

1. Go to www.factsurfer.com.

2. Enter "poison dart frogs" into the search box.

3. Click the "Surf" button and you will see a list of related Web sites.

With factsurfer.com, finding more information is just a click away.

Index

The images in this book are reproduced through the courtesy of: Martin Van Lokven/Minden Pictures, front cover; Thomas Marent/Getty Images, pp. 4-5, 20-21; Mark Moffett/Getty Images, pp. 6-7, 8-9; Konrad Wothe/Getty Images, pp. 10-11; Alfredo Maiquez/Photolibrary, pp. 12-13; B Holland/Getty Images, pp. 14-15; Robert Thompson/Nature Picture Library, pp. 16, 17; Joel Sartore/Getty Images, p. 19.

31901051916684